shadow.

self.

shadow.self.

Jayne Coots, Editor
Megan Nochi, Cover Design
Megan Nochi, Interior Book Design
Champagne Book Design, Book Formatting
Anonymous, Black Line Art Drawings

SHADOW. SELF. PLAYLIST

Smoke & Mirrors, RJD2

Sober, TOOL

everything i wanted, Billie Eilish

Popular Monster, Falling In Reverse

Street Spirit (Fade Out), Radiohead

Demons, Imagine Dragons

Human, Rag'n'Bone Man

Cassandra, Taylor Swift

Stubborn Love, The Lumineers

Scars, James Bay

Just Breathe, Pearl Jam

Midnight In A Perfect World, DJ Shadow

Soul To Take, Joe Arden

Control, Halsey

Time, NF

Not Going Back, Childish Gambino

DEDICATION

to the opposite of indifference

"I saw that, of the two natures that contended in
the field of my consciousness,
even if I could rightly be said to be either, it was
only because I was radically both."
—Robert Louis Stevenson,
The Strange Case of Dr. Jekyll & Mr. Hyde

"Civilisation is hooped together, brought
Under a rule, under the semblance of peace
By manifold illusion; but man's life is thought,
And he, despite his terror, cannot cease"
—William Butler Yeats, *Meru*

"And if I could, I'd get you the moon."
—Kina, *Get You The Moon*

CONTENTS

INTRODUCTION

Four months after my fifty-one-year-old mother lost her sub-lime battle with cancer, I went to see Judith Light star in a pro-duction of Margaret Edson's Wit. The play centers on Vivian Bearing, a fifty-year-old John Donne scholar dying of four-stage ovarian cancer. In the show, she wrestles with mortal-ity, legacy, and punctuation. Yes, punctuation! She spends lengthy moments on stage waxing and waning on the import of the commas, semicolons, and periods that fill the lines of Donne's poems. While navigating her painful end, she probes the pauses of poetry to find the most accurate representation of their form. In what order, and said in what precise way, do these words hold the most veracity?

When should we question?
When is it appropriate to exclaim?
When do we rest?

In one of the show's final moments, Ms. Light—who looked a great deal like my mother and shared the same pro-fession—comes to a final realization about what she feels is the right ending for Donne's most famous piece. Her eyes light up, she gets out of her antiseptic hospital bed, floats down center stage, and recites the final stanza as she imag-ines Donne intended it. "And Death—capital D—shall be no more—semicolon. Death—capital D—thou shalt die—ex-cla-mation point!"[1]

Those are some of her "last coherent lines."[2] A few minutes later, she goes Code Blue, but is listed as Do Not Resuscitate (DNR), so Vivian quietly dies. In a poetic stage send off, she removes her gown, stands naked in a flood of light, raises her hands to the rafters, and sighs triumphantly her final mortal breath. Blackout.

I cried. I convulsed. I felt the rawest parts of my recent grief flood back to the surface: that seven AM phone call in which my father stated, "Son, it's happened"; the expected coldness and surprising hardness of her dead cheek against my wet lips; the nothingness that accompanied the inevitable overwhelm of feeling so much, so fast.

But in these memories, I was not drowning. In these morbid reflections, I was not lost or scared. No. Witnessing this fictional story played out on stage, connecting person-ally to many pieces of the narrative—large and small—gave me strength. I felt something I hadn't felt in months.

I felt understood.
I felt seen.
I felt un-alone.

Knowing that somewhere in Atlanta was a schoolteacher/playwright who articulated these pieces of my reality, that she

---

1   Edson, Margaret. Wit : a Play. New York :Faber and Faber, 1999.

2   Edson, Wit.

could give voice to the feelings of a total stranger so specifically, made me feel powerful. It gave me armor. It made me buoyant against that torrent of pain. Rather than suffocating in sorrow, I felt, for the first time in a long time, as though I could float.

Alan Bennett expresses this sentiment beautifully in his play, The History Boys: "The best moments in reading are when you come across something—a thought, a feeling, a way of looking at things—which you had thought special and particular to you. Now, here it is, set down by someone else, someone you have never met, someone who is even long dead. And it is as if a hand has come out and taken yours."[3]

That evening at the Geffen Playhouse in Westwood, I felt a hand reach out and grasp mine. And I have held on tightly ever since.

I seek art during life's most significant moments—the weddings and funerals, the love, the loss, and the longing. Even during the quietest, most banal moments—the simple Tuesdays that hold so much taken-for-granted beauty that Emily Webb can't stand the reflection of it in the third act of Our Town—I seek art.

When words are not enough, I seek imagery. When feelings choke out reason, I crave metaphor. When I feel lost in a newfound joy or a bone-crushing sadness, poetry becomes

3   Bennett, Alan. The History Boys. London: Faber and Faber, 2004.

my map, my canvas, my guide. Creating it, consuming it, camouflaging myself inside of it.

Art is the human response to those moments, those emotions that catapult us beyond the quotidian. When how we feel pushes us past the couch cushions of comfort, when life creates spaces of ecstasy or grief, joy or sorrow, art is there to help us explain, help us understand. Sometimes art serves to challenge our beliefs, while other times, it provides peace as fundamental as the warmth of a fire or the satiation of a meal: the sufficiency of belonging, the strength and solace of knowing we are...un-alone.

What follows is a collection of recent poetry created during a period of my own wrestling. Many of these words act as a mirror to some of the very works of literature I adore. Some are my fictional imaginings of the heart of some of my favorite fictional characters. Others are attempts at self-portrait and self-reflection.

In the following pages, we dive into the macabre, break down the binary, embrace the dark, and face passionately that which can often terrify and frighten us psychologically.

Many of these poems are accompanied by hand-drawn, black-and-white illustrations created by an anonymous artist as a direct response to the words on the facing page. I strongly believe that art generates, inspires, and helps create more art. This partnership and the resultant haunting images celebrate and practice the symbiotic power of creation.

In rhymed verse, structured haiku, and open sentences, I have attempted not to explain or draw conclusions but to ask questions. These pieces attempt to explore earnestly the concept of duality, the juxtaposition of human feelings that often feel antithetical to each other, both potent though opposed. But they are not. They live constantly, vitally, in all of us at all times.

We create ourselves from our passions and cravings. We acknowledge those yearnings and seek to control some of those impulses as a reflection of how we perceive the community and world around us. But the person we present to that world is forever a changing byproduct of desire's push and pull on us.

They live metaphorically in our shadow; like our shadow, they are always there, brought into sharper focus and clarity when presented to the light. We can never run from nor effectively deny our shadow. Its existence and its impact are inevitable. The shadow is a part of the self, intrinsically linked to the sum of each of us. Rather than deny or ignore those impulses and urges, we can achieve a more authentic identity if, like Peter Pan, we mourn the loss of our shadow and celebrate with "wildest glee" when Wendy sutures the shadow back to the self.

Occasionally, we would do well to turn from the light and observe and acknowledge that shadow that trails us everywhere. Carl Jung, the Swiss psychotherapist who pioneered valuing our spiritual selves, had much to say about The Shadow.

"Unfortunately, there can be no doubt that man is, on the whole, less good than he imagines himself or wants to be. Everyone carries a shadow, and the less it is embodied in the individual's conscious life, the blacker and denser it is."[4]

Here, he introduces the concept of our shadow selves, these versions of us that we may not be willing to accept and acknowledge. But our willful ignorance of those shadow impulses does not make them go away; instead, it gives them density and weight within us. As an unacknowledged, unexplored part of self, it becomes like an anchor preventing our forward momentum, figuratively planting that shadow and rooting us in its place.

The shadow tree: the only plant that thrives on neglect.

Jung later goes on to identify that shadow as "the thing a person has no wish to be."[5] But our negative judgments of those desires, of that darker part of self, do not make them any less real. They may not be the vibrant colors of our ideal self or the optimistic, holistic desires of our striving self, but they are still parts of our true self.

When we face that shadow and acknowledge its presence in us and our lives, we begin the process of comprehension

---

4   Jung, C. G. Psychology and religion. New Haven, CT: Yale Univ, 1938.

5   Jung, Carl G. Collected Works of C.G. Jung. Volume 16, Collected Works of C.G. Jung, Volume 16 ; Practice of Psychotherapy. Princeton, NJ :Princeton University Press, 2014.

and negotiation that allows us to make more genuine choices: choices forged in the strength of dual purpose. The self acknowledges the shadow; the shadow lays itself before the self.

These pages reflect on and examine some of these ideas and ideals. Creating and engaging with art always fills me with strength and comfort. I hope a reader might find similar power and solace in its consumption.

If nothing else, I hope the following collection of words serves as that hand reaching out to hold another: a simple but necessary reminder that we are, you and I and all of us, un-alone.

Joe Arden
August 24, 2024

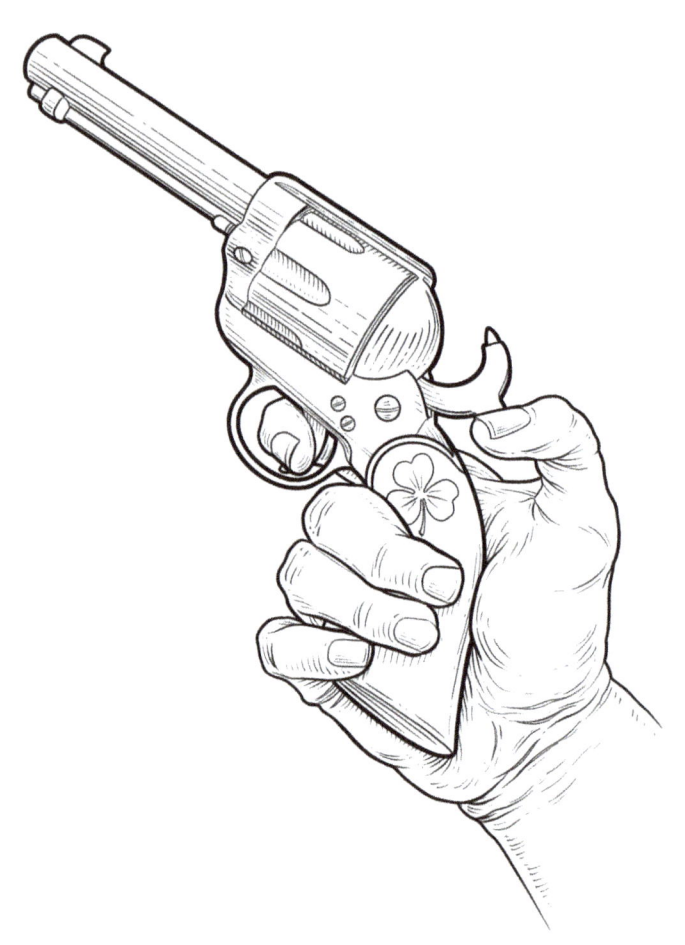

I

Trigger Warning

This story begins without a warning...
Observe though, my finger on the trigger.
Drape this dark tale in a cloak of mourning.
Feel now the onset of love's cold rigor.

Physic for it there is none. It will let
in and out the most complete consumptions.
Knew the road to trod, but the trek was not yet
over. Now life answers to assumptions.

Passion burning and instinct takes over,
No antidote to the vagrant fire that melts.
We found the unluckiest black clover,
Something inside wants this above all else.

    Last chance, turn around, if you must pretend.
    Cock back the hammer and watch love's cruel end.

i give you my heart
it's the only gift i have
i hope it's enough

II

Follow, Follow

i gaze at the you that faces the sun,
And marvel at how much you lock inside.
That visage you share seems like so much fun,
But i know all of the doubts that you hide.

Niggling thoughts dance with stinging remorse;
See you drown in a sea of pure darkness.
i'm with you, fear not, whatever the course
A partner of incomparable starkness.

Might think i follow to pester and fright,
But my purpose is more fundamental.
Woven into all your wrongs and your rights,
Though the world may judge harsh, i am gentle.

    Look down. i'm there. always watching. hello.
    Faithfully, tirelessly, your shadow.

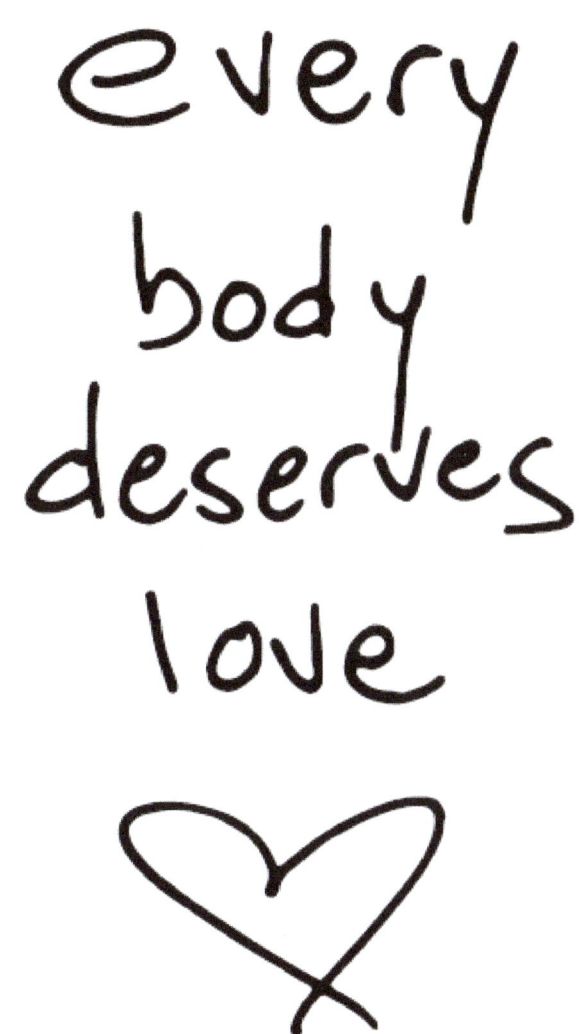

III

Monochrome

Been running from you for so many years,
Tenaciously, you always keep apace.
Rank miasma of desires and fears,
You won, 'fore i chanced to start up the race.

Rotten and buried, not for this world,
Swirling dark thoughts wrest total control.
The purr of that voice, coaxing me to unfurl.
Deny no part of my monochrome soul!

Persons aren't one word, we're adjectives more.
How we act; what we feel; cruel deception.
See the virgin—tis pity she's a whore.
Not you, oh you say...the single exception?

> Shadow tattoos itself into the skin.
> Self should not hide that which screams from within.

dew on the grass
cool night clings to the morning
like sparkling diamonds

despite your flaws? no.
it's the you those cracks create.
that's the reason why.

IV

Still Time

i am what i am, call me the devil.
Your words don't define the work that is done.
The picture remains when the dust settles.
Ink stains flesh and the needle never runs.

i paint my skin to tell my whole story:
A life full of choices made, loss and regret.
Absolutes blend into shades more hoary,
Still time in the game to place one more bet.

Find me dancing with spiders in the dark,
Spinning webs stronger than a string of lies.
The truth in the end never misses its mark,
In the hollow i cannot hear your cries.

    Reach out to me when all of it's written,
    For the lion too starts as a kitten.

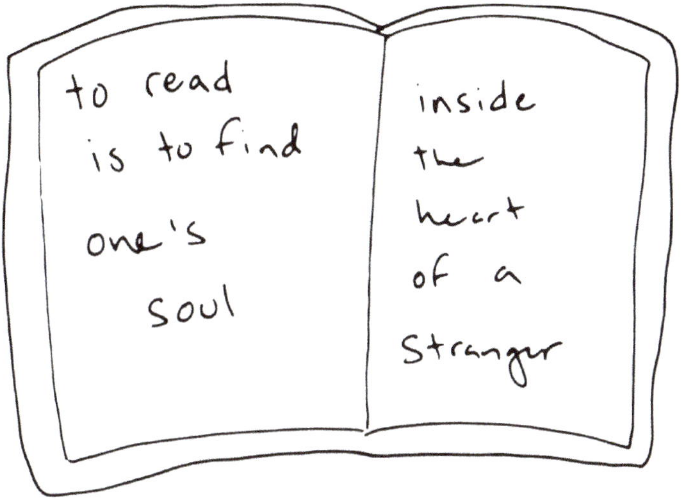

to read
is to find

one's
   soul

inside
the
heart
of a

stranger

V

Beneath the Black

Black is not a lack of color, but
rather the absence of light. What's hidden
in the darkness? Reveal it with a cut.
Slice ope' desire, ask it be bidden.

Dress up your passion in a three-piece suit
Hide your feelings beneath some refinement.
The costume you don speaks not to the truth
Your disguise only strictures confinement.

Free your true heart from the lies that you wear,
Unburden yourself. Come take off that cloak.
Wants burn brightly, they're yours alone to bear.
The rest of the blaze is nothing but smoke.

> That which is ebon does not mean empty.
> Onyx hides layers that yearn to tempt me.

i wish you could see
what i'm looking at right now
my eyes, your mirror

that lucky mirror
that hangs on your closet door.
sees you every day

VI

Always There

Can't see me in darkness; exposed by light.
Nocturnal, but only during daytime.
Sun gives me life, though a creature of night.
Simple paradox, an imperfect rhyme.

Follow close by, wherever feet tread,
Tied irrevocably tight to the whole.
Though many ignore and some too may dread,
Undeniably soldered to the soul.

Time and distance deftly alter the size.
Perspective can shift; slight change of angle.
Nothing can stifle those bestial cries,
Feelings impossible to strangle.

Truths often hide in the voiceless shadows.
Secretly holding what no one else knows.

if there's anything
I can do, don't hesitate...
your burden absolved

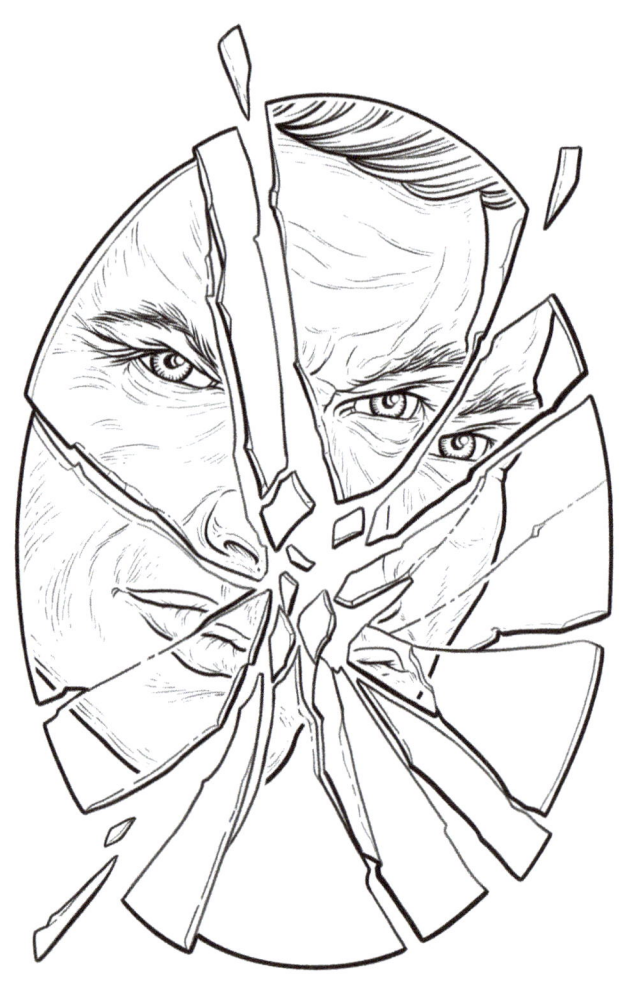

VII

Thanks, Friend

i should say thanks for showing me your heart,
Wish it hadn't taken this tragedy.
Guess it's true what they say: things fall apart.
Thought love is blind, as well, but now i see.

Suppose i owe you an apology.
Thoroughly confused, but i should have known.
Your face, a mirage, staring back at me.
Magic illusion: poof—i am alone.

Still, gave me strength in your deception,
'Cause i lived thinking you were by my side.
The easiest path—your true direction...
i've chosen another way; find a ride.

　　i thought i could count on you till the end;
　　Now you've shown me, you were never a friend.

Thank You/Thanks (Friend)

v.1
i thought i could count on you till the end
Now you've shown me, you were never a
friend.

2
Suppose i owe you an epilogy
~~these~~ (un)confused, but ~~guess~~ i should
have known
your face, a mirage, staring back
at me
magic illusion: puf. i am alone

1
i should say thanks for showing me your heart
Wish it hadn't taken this tragedy
to ~~terminate i should have known~~
~~It must be that you ~~missed~~~~
guess it's true what they say: my sight got par.
~~And i'm blind what someone can see~~
Thought love is blind as well, but now i see.

3
~~Still~~ you gave me strength in your description
~~because~~ i kept thinking you were by my side.
the easiest path ~~was~~ your ^true direction
i'm going another way; find a side.

VIII

a voice

Been left all alone with nothing but thoughts:
Thump thump, thump thump—disrupts the still silence.
Scrub, and scrub, and scrub: out, out you damn spots!
The mind writes symphonies of violins.

(violence)

Minor chords thrum darkly in the moonlight.
Come close now, i will tell you a story.
With deft swiftness, of an ignorant knight
Whose rash sword sends souls to purgatory.

Nothing to live for, yet something to die
for. Never take for granted the power
of words. Scream if you want, if you feel you must try.
Mute yelling portends an endless hour.

Never relinquish the sound of your voice,
Till the dark army comes and leaves you no

(choice.)

my blood and my skin
nurtured and tilled this soil
that produced no fruit

each star overhead
portends of worlds yet unknown...
imagine them all

IX

Ode to a Raindrop

I see you, little drop of rain, clinging
To that leaf. i wonder why you won't let
Go. What are you holding on for? Bringing
life to the soil below, your purpose met.

Imagine the power of succumbing,
Giving of yourself to the universe.
Transcendence of returning becoming
more than your burial after the hearse.

Look at you now, gravity takes over!
(Or perhaps it was you made the free fall.)
Your descent to that thirsty young clover,
A ballet to scare away death's grey pall.

    Little droplet, you answered the riddle.
    Living happens to all in the middle.

torrential downpour
caught without an umbrella
look up, a rainbow

rather than fret for
leaf's inevitable death
celebrate its color.
it's radiance brings comfort.
brief legacy, worthy end.

X

To JPS

i went to the grave where you're buried,
To honor your life and show you respect.
Forgive the impertinence, i tarried.
How much time have i spent on regret?

Choking vines and damp moss have outlived you,
But the words that you've shared linger on.
i wonder if time can erase you,
Mundanity crawls uncaring along.

Did you ponder the limits of free will
When you met life's inevitable brother?
Saw you something new from that hollow hill?
Tell me now whether hell is the other.

Existence uncaptured in shrine or tomb.
The tapestry of time woven to loom.

key to my jail cell
clutched firmly in my gaunt hand
but the lock's mouth laughs
from outside this prison door.
tortured by this useless key.

XI

Of Time

When we need it the most, it eludes us;
Seems Life forever retains the last laugh.
Each turn around the sun, it consumes us;
An invisible ghost we fight with wrath.

Minute by minute, hour by hour,
We feel it, though it touches not our skin.
A seed can bloom to a radiant flower,
Brief glimpse of beauty before death begins.

We can feel the whole world in a moment:
Thrill of an orgasm, cry or laughter.
But to capture it, steal it or own it,
Intemperate smoke clouds the hereafter.

> We all bow down, imposing throne of time.
> You're every word, an impossible rhyme.

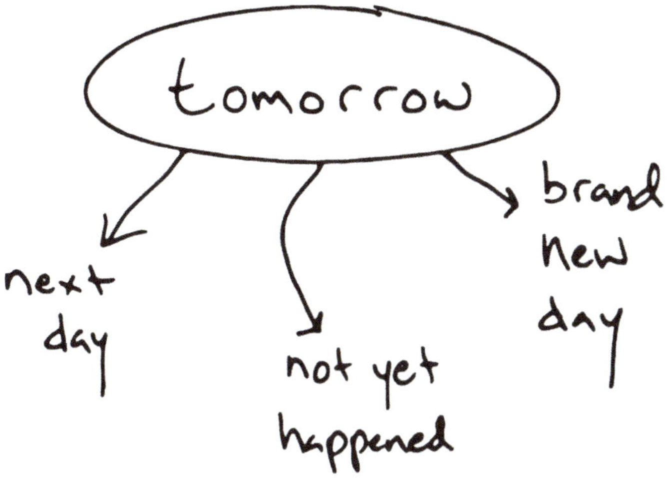

tomorrow

next day

not yet happened

brand new day

XII

After the Apple

The garden doesn't look the same after
the apple. The cave displays but shadows.
Razor blade pricks from the sound of laughter,
Judgement sentenced reason to the gallows.

Different doesn't mean worse, though. Just a chance
To view all with a nuanced perspective.
Torrential rain pours, i still choose to dance.
Reputation contra self: respective.

Actions speak volumes; your voice echoes mute.
Now i see what's behind Oz's curtain.
Sweet nectar of knowledge: forbidden fruit.
Of your negative thoughts, i'm now certain.

    Precious time that limits pure energy.
    Looking back perils all ahead of me.

tended that garden
with all of my willing heart
still no flowers born

lonely, neglected.
planted, then soon forgotten.
firmly grow those roots.

XIII

Ode to a Weed

Often i ponder the poor little weed:
A solitary thing of resilience.
In nature, it seems not to carry a need,
And its oft overlooked for its brilliance.

For think of the times and the places in life,
When something invasive can flourish.
Uprooted, maligned, never far from more strife,
i pull from the dandelion courage.

Easy to see where the damage is done,
When a weed overtakes a whole garden.
But marvel instead how hard fought it's won,
While pursued endlessly by hate's warden.

> Resistant strength of a thing unwanted;
> Dig deeply those roots; remain undaunted.

perfectly imperfect.

devastatingly human.

XIV

House, Fortified

i have made a house, fortified by pain:
Bricks dyed red from the color of my blood.
Sorrowful clouds threatening deadly rain,
Dug a moat with my hands. Bring on the flood.

i will plant flowers in resilient soil,
Water them daily with self-affirmed faith.
Malignant blight overcome by hard toil,
Marrow and essence will poison the wraith.

i will leave hope sitting in the window,
Warm and fresh like a homemade apple pie.
Smells of passion wafted by the willow,
Drowning out the bitter stench of a lie.

> Creation forged in the fire of love:
> Vultures can't capture the high-flying dove.

facing the sunrise:
yellow, orange, and crimson
possibilities

sat under a tree
in stillness for a season.
the crow came at last.

XV

Three Wise Monkeys

See no evil dancing seductively:
Avert thy gaze from poisonous action.
Closed eyes cannot punish destructively:
What's done in the dark boasts no refraction.

Hear no evil sings the true heart of gold.
Perfect pitch found within your siren song.
Listen not to the slanders that mold.
Rotten, misshapen sense of right and wrong.

Speak no evil, voiceless to desire
Choke suffering out, give malice no air.
Keep canary mouths shut, silent choir
Got something to say? Confess it in prayer.

> Triptych symbols reflecting dual meaning.
> Unknown sins from passion intervening.

Keep shining your light,
it will keep you warm.

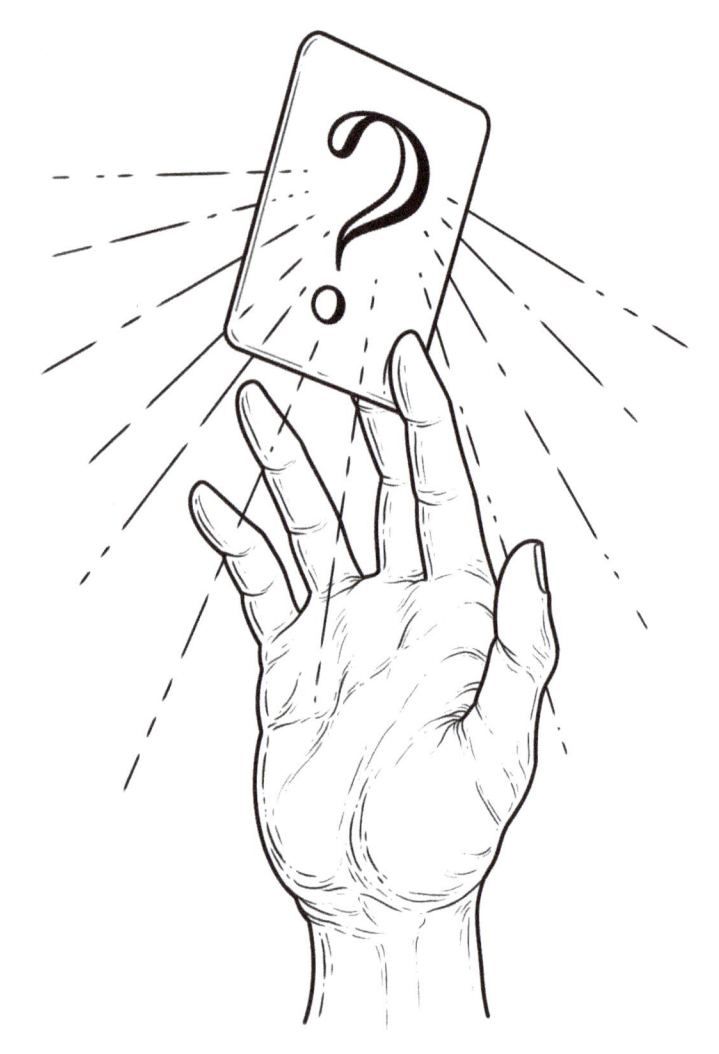

XVI

the lost sonnet

Silence speaks volumes in a world of noise,
Powerful echoes that shatter the din.
Misused words volleyed around like cheap toys
convincing none, of that which lies within.

Hearing is easy, now try to listen.
Senses are senseless when devoid of thought.
Eyes distracted by all that which glistens,
Focus the mind to find truth where thou ought.

Wander the world, seek all of its wonder.
In a bowl full of labels, choose mystery.
Watch curiosity burst asunder!
Write the present; they'll sing of your history.

    Skin often heals toughest under your scars.
    Trauma builds fortitude: pain's prison bars.

the absence of sound
is not quiet...noise within
the hardest to mute

aquamarine foam
persistently attacks shore
ocean's brutal teeth

XVII

Victor

My mind transfixed by a singular aim:
To create is my one true obsession.
Look at these fools play their laughable games.
Victory in the end: my possession.

Imagine a world where grief can abate,
Where sorrows sing softly, then...silent.
Some have judged this a malignant trait,
Benign my sharp aims, never violent.

See now the glorious act of creation!
Dedication my sole purpose has won.
But regret haunts this ugly mutation,
Endless remorse now for what i have done.

> Wanted to bring back a love that was mine.
> Seems i'm a monster, call me Frankenstein.

Sometimes, i wish
i saw
                    the me
that you see.

XVIII

That Man

Static electric passion, come undress
your desires before the cracked mirror.
Take in the vicious sight of a princess
in the arms of a monster. Can't hear her.

Drugged by the euphoria of longing,
Follow Charon down the muted river.
Around the bend, a new world dawning:
Open your mouth and let in the shiver.

Don't turn away from the magnet that pulls
you. Instead feel the power when you flip.
Nothing so frightening as a pack of wolves,
Save for that feral man whose passion grips.

    Take all of me in your infinite love;
    i would burn the world down for you, my dove.

feathery kisses
all along your pebbled flesh
the wind whispers love

honeysuckle bud
that i plucked in early spring
you were delicious

XIX

Fantasy

i would, of course, if i had more time, but
what could we make with a few more brushes
of pink sky? For night slices a deep cut,
And we're left with black blood as it rushes.

Wait for me then in your goose-down prison, and
think of me in the stillness to follow.
Reach out from your mind and take my true hand,
Hope the empty clasp doesn't feel hollow.

Find me in dreams where i silently roam,
No one can purloin imagination.
Shadowy king of a silver unknown,
Subconscious love beckons transmutation.

Existing in the realm of fantasy
Makes no less real what no one else can see.

your holy screams are
my nectar. pour them on me.
show me how it feels.

the way you shake makes
me believe in religion.
speaking in tongues.

XX

Unmasked

Though some remain hidden, we all wear masks.
What's inside the you you keep from the world?
Answer all the questions that no one asks.
It's just the two of us, now come unfurled.

The power you've hidden underneath glows,
Who told you to bury your beautiful?
Every scar tells me what your body knows,
Your presence to me is immutable.

Love grown from the heart of the darkest place,
What blooms inside your locked shadow garden?
A light cracks through from a glimpse of your face,
Take my name, they're not your words to pardon.

    Carry me with you wherever you go;
    Neither space nor time can steal what we know.

numbers may be few,
though the impact deeply felt:
true friendship's power.

do you see that bug?
stuck on his back, legs flailing.
but if he could flip!

XXI

Together

i have climbed the mountain of enduring
sadness. Sisyphus and his rock passed by.
Gray clouds rolled in, my vision obscuring.
Lonely as i am, together we cry.

You are my specter of the night. Feeling
the ache of my emptiness. And in so
doing, lifting my body from kneeling.
Enough my persistence to know you know.

Please never question the power of your
presence, the impact you have on my life.
Weight of the world presses on evermore,
But the burden cleaved by your loving knife.

    Some trials feel like they're too much to bear.
    Alone they may be, but not when you're there.

pick up
those
shattered
dreams
and
watch them
'sparkle'

XXII

Not a Rainbow

A rainbow can only shine through cracked glass.
This isn't true, but i want it to be.
Trying to say something poignant, alas,
Metaphor ruined by reality.

Turns out that glass only needs to bend
For white light to filter out in color.
It helped me to think of how i might mend.
Pain with a purpose feels somehow duller.

Prisms take stabs of light through diffusion,
Softens one point of force into several.
This prison, these bars: only illusion.
Scars endure, though the hurt be ephemeral.

> Found solace in here to cope with trauma.
> This darkness: no period...a comma.

made space in my heart
in a room with no more walls
for a boundless love

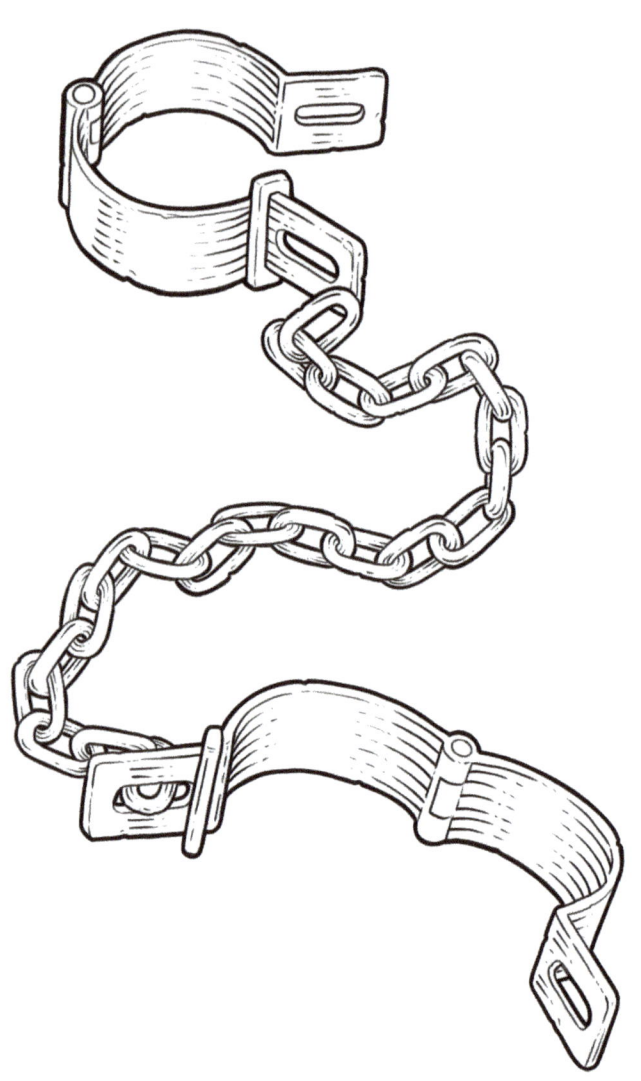

XXIII

Untethered

Built an impenetrable December:
Winter's torture palace bathed in bloodstains.
But you forgot what I always remember,
Man is free and everywhere he's in chains.

Soundproof walls spackled by caustic contempt,
Underestimated power of screams.
Brittleness fractured your feeble attempt,
Confinement combated by diamond cut dreams.

Drowning and choking, head under water,
Resilient breath of air turns quickly thc tide.
Shackles now opened, my turn for slaughter.
Malignant venture to kill me has died.

    Scene from the dungeon, the view from the grave.
    Empty the coffin, no longer a slave.

Nothing Ends.

ACKNOWLEDGEMENTS

i acknowledge pain.
i acknowledge pleasure.
i acknowledge passion.
i acknowledge purpose.

i acknowledge anyone and everyone who has brought any measure of these into my life, by varying degrees and for myriad reasons. i acknowledge each and every one of you and the physical, emotional, and psychological impact you've had on me and my creative work.

Nothing happens in a vacuum. No one is an island unto themselves. In creation, there is never simply a 'me'; always a 'we'.

This work of creation was shepherded into existence with the assistance of not just many people but every person with whom i've interacted.

Regardless of interest or intent, your influence and impact on my life has, in ways understood and others unknown, molded this piece into the work that lay before us today.

i acknowledge the existence of truth and the truth of existence.

These words are mine; This world is ours.
Creation belongs to us all.

ABOUT THE AUTHOR

As a voice actor, Joe Arden's deeply emotional performances and character connectivity have made him a fan favorite. Over the years, he has brought hundreds of memorable characters to life. Joe's passion for the art of storytelling have propelled into more areas of creation as an author, a musical artist, and a performer.

His solo writing debut, *The Chameleon Effect*, was shortlisted by Audible's Editorial Staff as "one of the Best Audiobooks of 2022," earned an Earphones Award, and was voted one of the "Top 100 Romance Audios of All Time."

Joe's entrepreneurial spirit and thirst for creativity can be seen almost daily in his original works and community engagement inside The Audio Attic. On the stage, on the page, and in the booth, Joe finds places and spaces to share his love for words, language, and human experiences.

STAY CONNECTED

To join a community of lovers of love
and celebrate all things storytelling,
check out **The Audio Attic** :

patreon.com/JoeArden

For exclusive merch, info on upcoming live appearances,
and much more, visit :

TheRealJoeArden.com

SOCIALS

@TheRealJoeArden

BOOKISH

www.bookbub.com/authors/joe-arden

www.goodreads.com/author/show/20682028.Joe_Arden